Through the Fence

D1523901

Contents

Abby, Nate, and Josh Go Exploring. . 2

Another World. 8

Meeting Titu. 14

The Rescue. 20

Home Again. 30

Written by Janette Johnstone
Illustrated by Colin Dowden

Abby, Nate, and Josh Go Exploring

It was a warm afternoon. Three young friends were sitting on the roof of their apartment building. School had only just finished and already the three were bored.

Josh sighed. "What are we going to do?"

"Let's go skateboarding in the park," suggested Nate.

"Nah, that's not exciting," said Abby. "I know, why don't we go exploring? I'm reading this great book about an explorer who discovered a lost city. It's really exciting!"

"That sounds great, but where are we going to explore that we haven't been before?" asked Nate.

"Well," replied Abby, "you know that old empty house on the other side of the park, the one with the high fence around it that everyone says is strange? Why don't we go exploring there?"

"I don't know," said Josh doubtfully, "people say strange things happen there, and anyway, the fence is too high to climb over."

"It's all right, I know how to get in," said Abby. "The other day when I went shopping, I went past the old house. I found a loose board in the fence. We'll be able to squeeze through."

"OK, let's go!" said Nate suddenly.

So the three friends raced down the stairs to the street and across the park until they came to the old empty house. No one had lived in it for years.

"It looks spooky," said Josh. "I'm not sure this is really a good idea."

"Don't be so scared," Abby said. "Come on, I'll go first."

Abby tugged at the loose board.

"Come on," she said as she wiggled through the gap and disappeared. Nate squeezed through after her.

Once Abby and Nate had gone through the fence, Josh felt nervous. Everything was suddenly very quiet and Josh wondered what they had found on the other side.

5

Josh stood for a moment, deciding if he was brave enough to follow.

"Nate," he called, "Nate, wait for me!"

There was no answer. Now Josh felt even more nervous, but he wanted to be with his friends, so he pushed his way into the gap in the fence. He was bigger than Abby and Nate, and his pants caught on a nail. He couldn't move. He was stuck.

"I'll just have to push as hard as I can," he said to himself, and he pushed hard with his feet.

Suddenly there was a ripping sound as his pants tore on the nail and Josh fell through the gap. Everything went black. He had a strange feeling of falling, so he closed his eyes tight.

Another World

After what seemed like ages, he carefully opened his eyes. Instead of lying on the lawn of the old house, he was lying in a rocky field. Abby and Nate were sitting nearby waiting for him.

"Where are we?" Josh asked them.

"We're in misty mountains somewhere," replied Abby. "We must be really high up because we can nearly touch these clouds."

"But where are we?" asked Josh again.

"We don't know," replied Nate.

Just then, the mist lifted a little and the friends could see that they were surrounded by the icy peaks of other mountains. It was magical, but also frightening.

"Look!" said Abby. "Look! There's a flight of steps going down the mountain."

"Look, the steps head back up to that city over there with the buildings made of stone blocks," said Nate.

"And there are some people, too," said Josh with relief. "We're not alone. I thought we were all alone in some strange place with no way to get home."

"And look!" said Nate excitedly, pointing to the steps. "There's a boy over there. Come on, let's go and talk to him before he goes away."

Carefully, the friends walked over to where the boy was standing on the steps. He was holding a stick in one hand and waving to the friends to come over with the other hand.

Meeting Titu

"We're lost," Abbey said shyly. "Can you tell us where we are?" Then she added politely, "What is your name?"

"My name is Titu. I'm named after a famous Inca chief. I live in Machu Picchu," he said proudly, pointing down the side of the mountain to the city.

The children stared at Titu in amazement.

Titu stared back. "Who are you?" he asked. "And why are you wearing those strange clothes? Where do you come from?"

"We come from a very big city," Abby replied, but she didn't try to explain how they got there.

"I read about Machu Picchu at school," Nate said excitedly. "It was a lost city. The Incas lived there over 400 years ago. It was found again in 1911 by an American explorer named Hiram Bingham. I think we've fallen into the past!"

"You mean my city is going to be lost?" asked Titu. "How can that be?"

"We must have gone back through time when we climbed through the hole in the fence," said Abby, ignoring Titu's question.

"But how are we going to get home again?" cried Josh.

No one answered him.

"So, how did you get here?" asked Titu.

Abby, Nate, and Josh explained as much as they could about what had happened. Titu asked a lot of questions about their lives. He didn't seem frightened, just interested. Abby, Nate, and Josh asked Titu many questions, too. They wanted to know about life in the city of Machu Picchu.

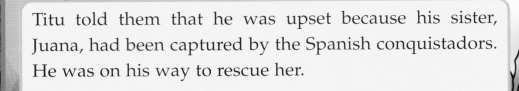

Titu told them that he was upset because his sister, Juana, had been captured by the Spanish conquistadors. He was on his way to rescue her.

"Can we come, too?" asked Nate.

"We could help," said Abby.

Josh, not wanting to be left behind, agreed to go with them.

"Tell me more about what you learned at school," said Titu.

"In 1532, the Spanish conquistadors landed in South America, looking for gold," said Abby. "Our books say they were really cruel people."

"Yes, they are cruel," agreed Titu. "Juana is a prisoner at their camp next to the Urubamba River." He pointed down into the valley.

"Isn't that a long way down the mountain?" asked Josh.

"Yes, it is," replied Titu, "but I know an easy way. It won't take us very long if we start now."

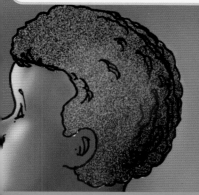

The Rescue

Titu led the way. Nate and Abby followed. Josh fell behind, and he couldn't help thinking that they would never reach the bottom of the mountain. It was rocky, slippery, and very steep. Josh wished he could just lie down and have a rest, but he didn't want to be on his own. So he hurried to catch up to the others.

Suddenly, near the bottom of the mountains, Titu stopped, turned around, and held his finger to his lips.

"We're close to the conquistadors' camp now, so be very quiet," he whispered as he led the way.

"Look," whispered Abby. "Is that Juana over there, tied to that tree?"

"Yes," replied Titu. " That's my sister. Now we've found her, we have to find a way to free her."

There were five conquistador soldiers standing near Juana talking to each other. Each soldier had bright red pants which tucked into their long boots. They each wore a metal helmet. They carried weapons and they did not look friendly!

Josh was very frightened.

"Let's go," he begged. "Let's get out of here before they capture us as well." But no one was listening to him.

Titu waved with his arm for them all to move back. When he was sure they could not be heard, he whispered, "We need a plan."

"I have a plan," said Abby. "Listen."

She whispered for a few minutes, and they all agreed that it was a good plan.

Quickly and quietly, Titu went to the soldiers' horses and untied them. Then he frightened them by waving his arms so that they galloped away.

"What's that noise?" shouted one of the soldiers.

"What's happened to the horses?" shouted another, starting to run after them.

"A boy's let them loose! Come on, let's get him!" shouted another soldier.

While the soldiers were chasing Titu and the horses, Abby and Nate crept up to the tree where Juana was tied. Nate used his pocketknife to saw through the ropes.

"Don't be afraid, Juana," whispered Abby. "We're here with your brother to rescue you. Be very quiet until Nate can cut the ropes, and then run as fast as you can with us. Do you understand?"

Juana nodded her head. Nate was still sawing at the ropes when they heard a whistle. It was Josh, who was standing guard.

"Quick, somebody must be coming," whispered Abby, just as one of the soldiers appeared at the other end of the clearing.

When the soldier saw what was happening, he gave a loud shout and ran over to them. As he crossed the clearing, Josh threw a stone in front of him. The surprised soldier tripped and fell to the ground.

"Quick, Nate!" yelled Josh, "before more of them come."

Nate sawed frantically with his small pocketknife until he had cut through the last strands of rope. When she was free, Juana jumped to her feet and ran off into the trees. Abby, Nate, and Josh ran as fast as they could behind her as another soldier joined in the chase, waving his sword in the air.

"This way! Follow me!" shouted a voice. It was Titu.

"This way! In here!" he shouted, as he pulled a large branch aside to reveal a cave entrance. "We can hide in here. Quick!" The children quickly scrambled into the cave.

"Will we be safe in here?" panted Josh loudly.

"We'll be safe if you keep quiet," Titu said softly, with a smile, so that Josh would know he wasn't angry.

They all held their breath as the soldiers crashed around outside. After what seemed like forever, everything was quiet again.

"What are we going to do now?" whispered Josh. "How are we going to get out of here?"

"We'll wait a little longer," replied Titu. "When it's dark, we'll climb back up the mountain to the safety of Machu Picchu."

When the sun had set, the children quietly left the cave and climbed back up the mountain. It was dark, so they had to go very very slowly.

Home Again

It took them all night to get back to Machu Picchu, but when they finally got there, the people treated them like heroes for rescuing Juana.

"But how are we going to get home?" Josh asked.

"I'll take you back to the field where you arrived," said Titu. "We'll look for the way back in the field."

So Titu led them back up the steps to the field.

"Those bushes look much darker than they should be," he said to Abby, Nate, and Josh. "I bet if you push your way in there you'll get home again."

"Goodbye, my new friends, and thank you," said Titu.

Abby led the way as she had before. She pushed into the bushes, and before she knew it, she came out by the loose board in the fence of the old empty house. Nate and Josh followed her.

"No one will ever believe us when we tell them," said Josh.

Abby smiled. "Where shall we go exploring tomorrow?" she asked.

"Nowhere!" replied Nate and Josh together.